D1133229

Currency Methuen Plays:
series three
General editor: Katharine Brisbane

Coralie Lansdowne Says No
a play by Alexander Buzo

Preface by Ken Horler

The Currency Press, Sydney
Eyre Methuen, London
1974

First published in 1974
by Currency Methuen Drama Pty Ltd,
301 Kent Street, Sydney,
New South Wales, 2000.

Printed by John Sands Pty Ltd,
Halstead Press Division.

National Library of Australia
card number & ISBN 0 86937 025 1 (cased edition)
          ISBN 0 86937 024 3 (limp edition)

For Merelyn

Kevin Howard as Stuart and Jude Kuring as Coralie
in the Nimrod Street Theatre production.
Photograph by Jan Dalman

Preface   The title is a big tease since Coralie Lansdowne finally does say yes. Not, however, with a bang, but with a whimper. Surrounded by the detritus of the wedding feast, the high flying bird is left with her poet and public servant, and possibly the life in the suburbs against which she has been railing throughout the play.

Since the play was first seen at the Adelaide Festival in March 1974 audiences and critics have been divided over Coralie's choice. For those who respond solely to the naturalistic aspects of the play, identifying too closely with Coralie's problem, the end is a cop-out. For those who see through the silicon casing to Coralie's soft centre, the final "You'll do" is the only possible resolution of her dilemma.

Coralie is a bitch who lashes her three suitors (and herself) with a laser-like wit. But when the bitch shows that she is vulnerable and starts to unzip her very real fears, some audiences are reluctant to let go of their self-sufficient Women's Libber, content with seeing only the author's shafts aimed at fashionable protest, film buffs and wine snobs. This provides a challenge to a director and his leading actress. As Coralie, Jude Kuring in the original production seized on the wit, the languor and the emotional shifts in the play with great energy and intelligence.

Earlier plays had shown Alexander Buzo's skill in writing parts for women. But neither Sandy in **Rooted** nor Susan in **Tom** held the centre as firmly as Coralie. Of the current Australian playwrights, probably only Peter Kenna can portray women as well, although his earth mother figures inhabit a different world from Buzo's sometime art teacher stoking up on Southern Comfort. Coralie's revolt derives from her fear of turning thirty. This fear is skilfully substantiated by the arrival of Anne Coleman, who announces that she is expecting her third child. She is only on stage for about 25 minutes, but in that brief space she moves credibly from persiflage to suicide, thanks to the sureness of the writing complemented in the first production by the fine playing of Berys Marsh. (In the first draft Anne killed herself by an overdose of pills. It is interesting that in the present version she is destroyed by the sea, to which Coralie herself is so drawn.)

It is endemic to Alexander Buzo's dramatic style that he does not allow his audience great sympathy for his

5

characters. Nevertheless in **Coralie Lansdowne Says No** he has created the most nearly rounded set of people of all his plays. We are prevented from responding even to Coralie with direct sympathy by the character's own capacity for self-analysis: like many of Alexander Buzo's most successful characters, she is articulate beyond the demands of naturalistic theatre. Finding a form to accommodate both the naturalistic and non-naturalistic levels in the play was an important job in rehearsals. For example: Jill forces a showdown with Stuart whom she has invited to stay. On one level there is a very funny dialogue touching on the cult of the Bonsai, poetic pretension and so on. Under the text there is an emotional claim being strongly asserted and resisted, a struggle which could casily swamp the scene. The economy and allusiveness of the dialogue suggested a style of playing which was light, fast and indirect. Another example is Coralie's sudden convulsion at the end of the play, which cannot be satisfactorily explained as a symptom of food poisoning or other such disorder. We treated it as a rejection of Stuart Morgan and his world (globus hystericus, maybe), an interpretation which makes sense of Dr Salmon's exit line, "That's the least of your worries."

In trying to achieve the appropriate form we found it valuable to focus on three strong images which recur throughout the play. The first was the physical image of Coralie's eyrie high above the beach. The second was deformity; Coralie herself says: "Everyone around here is rich and deformed. It's freaky territory—lots of Mercedes and wheelchairs." And this concern for the emotionally crippled continues to the end. The third was the image of pursuit, ambush and capture as each of the men lays siege to Coralie.

In **Coralie Lansdowne Says No**, Alexander Buzo's brilliant and economical dialogue is imbued with an empathy for a certain type of Australian woman which gives a new dimension to his comic writing.

Ken Horler   June 1974

6

ALEXANDER BUZO was born in Sydney in 1944, the son of a civil engineer. He was brought up in Armidale, New South Wales, and educated at The Armidale School and later at the International School of Geneva. In 1965 he graduated B.A. from the University of New South Wales.

After a workshop production of his first play at the New Theatre, Sydney, in 1967, he came to the notice of a national public in 1968 when the Old Tote Theatre Company presented his one-act play, **Norm and Ahmed**, directed by Jim Sharman. This was followed by **Rooted** (1968), **The Front Room Boys** (1969) and **The Roy Murphy Show** (1970). Of these early comedies it was **Rooted** which took Buzo's name abroad. Its first American production was by the Hartford Stage Company in 1972; it had its English premiere at the Hampstead Theatre Club in 1973. **The Front Room Boys** has also been produced in London, and is published in German as **Antipoden** (Universal Edition Schauspiel 1972, translated by Renate and Martin Esslin).

In 1972-3, Alexander Buzo was resident playwright with the Melbourne Theatre Company. During this time the MTC premiered his historical play, **Macquarie**; his comedy **Tom**; and his adaptation of Ibsen's **An Enemy of the People**, set in Victoria and titled **Batman's Beach-head**. **Tom** and **Macquarie** were awarded the Australian Literature Society's gold medal for the best work by an Australian writer in 1972. **Tom** received its American premiere at the Arena Stage, Washington, on 19th December 1973, directed by Alan Schneider.

Coralie Lansdowne Says No was first performed at the Adelaide Festival of 1974. It is the sixth play by Alexander Buzo to be published.

Alexander Buzo now lives in Sydney. He is married and has a daughter.

CORALIE LANSDOWNE SAYS NO
by Alexander Buzo

The author wishes gratefully to acknowledge that **Coralie Lansdowne Says No** was written with the financial assistance of The Literature Board of the Australian Council for the Arts.

Coralie Lansdowne Says No was first performed by the Nimrod Street Theatre Company at Theatre 62, Adelaide, on 9th March 1974 with the following cast:

PETER YORK	Robert Newman
CORALIE LANSDOWNE	Jude Kuring
JILL LANSDOWNE	Donna Akersten
STUART MORGAN	Kevin Howard
PAUL COLEMAN	John Orcsik
ANNE COLEMAN	Berys Marsh
DR SALMON	Lloyd Casey

Setting designed by Kevin Brooks
Directed by Ken Horler

CHARACTERS:

PETER YORK, 44, solicitor. Urbane, handsome, good-natured. Black eye-patch over one eye.

CORALIE LANSDOWNE, 29, former art-teacher. A big girl with a dominating manner and a loud, coarse laugh. She moves quickly and lithely, and is attractive on her own terms.

JILL LANSDOWNE, 24, government administrator, CORALIE's sister. Plain, reserved, determined.

STUART MORGAN, 28, poet and public servant. Small, unhurried, naive, purposeful. Ineffectual in manner. At least three inches shorter than CORALIE.

PAUL COLEMAN, 32, businessman. Good looking, strongly built, gregarious.

ANNE COLEMAN, 30, housewife. Pretty, ragged, frail, English.

DR SALMON, middle-aged doctor with one artificial leg.

SETTING:

The action takes place in the living-room/sun-room of a large modern house high above the sea in the Bilgola-Palm Beach area north of Sydney. There is a large tree which grows up through the ceiling in centre stage. Towards the front there are a rounded sofa and chairs; at the right, a transparent staircase going up to a landing. There are two doors facing front on the landing. The kitchen is off, up left. Glass doors lead off right and left to banana groves and a path going steeply down to the beach. The only blemish in otherwise beautiful surroundings is a bar, down right.
It is summer.

SCENE ONE

Monday evening, about 8.30 p.m. Very gloomy twilight. Silence. PETER YORK *enters left through the glass door.*

PETER: Coralie?

(Pause.)

Coralie?

(He turns on the light and goes towards the staircase. He stops and examines something on the floor. CORALIE LANSDOWNE *comes out of the upstairs door right, wearing jeans and a blouse. She yawns and stretches.)*

CORALIE: Hello, Peter.
PETER: What a mess.
CORALIE: Thank you.
PETER: On the floor. Just look at it. The remains of my crab.
CORALIE: That bloody dog. No class. Once a scavenger . . .

*(*PETER *gets newspaper, sponge and a broom and cleans up the mess.* CORALIE *comes slowly down the stairs.)*

PETER: It was a beautiful concoction—boiled crab on a field of risotto with pineapple couchant round the perimeter. Crossed pincers and a Latin motto in parsley. What a creation! I had my children visiting for the day. I bought the crab at the markets on Friday and cooked it myself. Daddy the chef.
CORALIE: They probably wouldn't have liked it.
PETER: Probably not. Anyway, how are you?
CORALIE: Sleepy. There's only one thing to do with the stormy Monday blues and that's sleep 'em off.
PETER: I saw the lights on upstairs. I thought you were going to a seance at that clairvoyant's place this evening.
CORALIE: It was cancelled because of unforeseen circumstances.
PETER: Coralie!
CORALIE: *(grinning)* Sorry. No, actually, I've given it up.

13

I've been sleeping for, oh, for hours. Just sleeping. *(Seeing herself in the mirror)* Yuk! What's that?

PETER: You look all right to me.

(He takes the newspapers, etc. out to the kitchen.)

CORALIE: I'm looking at a piece of flotsam with a skin condition. Who are you talking about? God, it's hot. Would you like a drink?

PETER: *(off)* I'll have a scotch, thanks.

CORALIE: All I've got is Southern Comfort.

(PETER comes back from the kitchen.)

PETER: Doesn't that belong to your American friend?

CORALIE: He bequeathed it to me, along with the house.

PETER: So you've said, but did he mean you could drain the lot?

CORALIE: Carte blanche. Now do you want some Comfort or not?

PETER: Thanks.

(CORALIE mixes drinks at the bar.)

CORALIE: You know, there must be more to whoredom than a mansion with ocean views and a cellarful of Southern Comfort.

PETER: Sounds like beginner's luck.

CORALIE: I'd never had an affair with anyone like him. All my friends, i.e. the dog, were horrified. A square, middle-aged American businessman—undoubtedly a CIA agent or at the very least an IT&T spy.

PETER: Did you enjoy the affair? Was it exciting?

CORALIE: It wasn't unpleasant. I was about to break it off when he said he was going back to America and would I look after the house. Would I! I was unemployed, doing nothing, which still beats teaching art to recalcitrant yobs. The Renaissance. Who wants to know about it at Marrickville Girls' High? Contraception and how to make a pound of mince last a week'd be more to the point. Because it's in a working class area no one in the Government or the Education Department gives a bugger. It took me over a year to get a kiln for the art room and I was supposed to be teaching them pottery. How's your Southern Comfort?

PETER: Delightful. You certainly fell on your feet. I'll have to look around for a well-heeled American divorcee. She'd have to be about seventy, I suppose, for the chemistry to work.

CORALIE: What chemistry?

PETER: Sugar daddies and mummies have to be older than you. *(Quickly)* Not that age differences mean a great deal.

CORALIE: As long as they've got the loot, who cares how old they are? There, now I sound more like a whore.

PETER: You've done very well.

CORALIE: *(looking around)* It's not a bad place.

PETER: The tree is of course fabulous. And the view.

CORALIE: Yes, I can see the Pacific Ocean, and the sand, and the banana trees, and those porcine developers gouging bloody great welts out of the landscape and throwing up those horrendous erectile tunnels.

PETER: Indignation's an amazing quality. Amazing.

(Pause.)

I also like the silence. Which is of course the same next door. Particularly as I'm on my own. Which you are, too.

CORALIE: Yes, it's quiet, except for the boom and drawl of the surf and the cars on the main road and also this humming sound I hear from time to time. Do you ever hear it?

PETER: No.

CORALIE: Oh. Well, maybe I'm up myself. By the way, this arrived for you today while you were at work. The delivery man left it with me.

(She hands him a package. He unwraps it.)

PETER: Oh yes. *(Holding up a wooden board)* I ordered this to mount a silver plate. Thanks. You're a good neighbour.

CORALIE: My pleasure.

PETER: Coralie, I thought I might—we are alone in the house?

CORALIE: Of course we're alone.

PETER: I saw a girl on your terrace this morning.

CORALIE: That's my sister Jill. She's down from Canberra for a few days. If you've ever lived in Canberra you'd know

why. What a dull town. Full of boring tarantulas and their barracuda wives.

PETER: Oh. Well, anyway, I wanted to ask you if, you see, I'm a member of the Australia Party, and they're having a bit of a do over in Castlecrag and I wondered if—it's on Saturday week—and, would you like to come with me?

CORALIE: Well, uh, thanks, I don't know.

PETER: It should be quite interesting.

CORALIE: I'll think it over.

PETER: Okay.

(Pause.)

CORALIE: This bloody heat. I'm going to put a bit more Comfort in my ice. Like some?

PETER: I'll get them.

(He goes to the bar and mixes the drinks.)

(Smiling) I like the bar.

CORALIE: Isn't it a shocker? But I love the rest of the house—for what it is.

PETER: It's beautiful. But the bar is a giveaway. Love these vinyl sausages.

CORALIE: Yes, presumably they're meant to soften the fall of pissed midgets.

PETER: Millionaires think of everything.

(They laugh.)

CORALIE: He's not a bad bloke. Really.

PETER: I'm sure he's very sensitive.

CORALIE: Don't be a bastard.

PETER: Where's Jill?

CORALIE: Down at the beach.

PETER: It's not the safest place at night. Not these days. There was a rape down there last summer.

CORALIE: Yes, Jill has high hopes.

PETER: I can't imagine you with a family. Are your parents alive?

CORALIE: Only my mother. I saw her yesterday, actually. We had a terrible blue. She said—I believe the topic of conversation was thrift—she said: "A paper bag is a paper bag"; and I muttered something about self-evident truths

and she belted me one, expostulating all the while about some kind of come-uppance I'm apparently soon to receive. What a harridan! The full Jannali fishwife. I don't know how I coped.

PETER: She was probably trying to give you some advice.

CORALIE: Yes, but it's always the same. When I was nineteen she'd say: "Why don't you wear a dress, Coralie, you'd look so much nicer." Now I'm twenty-nine and she says: "You're always in jeans, for Christ's sake buy a dress before it's too late." She's immutable. In this transient age of flux and oscillation my mother stays exactly the same in her own little cobwebbed harbour.

PETER: You don't listen to advice.

CORALIE: Nope.

PETER: That's something about you young people that I—

CORALIE: Young? What do you mean, young? I'm twenty-nine. In a few months my youth will be at an end.

PETER: Thirty? Is that old?

CORALIE: Thirty is death. I want to spend my thirtieth birthday in Bali on a beach surrounded by black candles.

PETER: You lot fascinate me. You drift through life, aimless, rootless—

CORALIE: That I have never been.

PETER: Flippant, smart-arsed,

CORALIE: I'm sorry.

PETER: Apologetic,

CORALIE: Oh shut up.

(She laughs.)

PETER: *(smiling)* But you see what I mean.

CORALIE: Yes, I suppose to your legal mind I do seem a drifter. A vagrant. A kept de facto or whatever.

PETER: A bum living a transient life.

CORALIE: I thrive on transience. The shortest book in the world, shorter even than *Italian War Heroes* or *What's On In Canberra* is a slim volume entitled *The Prospects for Coralie Lansdowne.*

PETER: Maybe when you turn thirty you'll renounce this life of aimless leisure.

CORALIE: Oh, it's not that I'm idle. I have my interests—I cultivate bananas on the front slope, I collect and play old

Lesley Gore and Brenda Lee forty-fives—*You Don't Own Me* is a personal favourite—I spend every morning on the beach, I read in the afternoon, I sleep—alone—at night. As far as I'm concerned, everything is sunshine, lollipops and rainbows—comparatively.

PETER: Transience, by definition, can't last forever.

CORALIE: You want to bet.

PETER: This is an atypical period in your life. You've been awarded a six-month respite, half of which is gone.

CORALIE: What do you mean, six months? I've had a twenty-nine-year respite.

PETER: Look, about this party . . .

CORALIE: Don't tell me you want to "date" me.

PETER: Well . . .

CORALIE: You want to be my "escort", is that it?

PETER: Do I detect a "back off" tone in your voice?

CORALIE: More of a "don't rush it", I would say.

PETER: You think I'm pushing you?

CORALIE: Yes, just let things develop in their own time.

PETER: Things don't just develop. They have to be nudged along.

CORALIE: You're starting to sound almost urgent. A mountain brook should not contain scarlet water.

PETER: You broke first. You came round that night and sobbed your heart out. I couldn't get rid of you.

CORALIE: Yes, but I slept on your sofa and wanted nothing else.

PETER: That doesn't matter.

CORALIE: It still doesn't.

(Pause.)

Relax, Peter, and wait for it.

(The phone rings. CORALIE answers it.)

The Lansdowne residence. Yes. Who? Paul? Oh. Oh, fine. Uh . . . how are you? Great. Oh, are you? Yes, of course. Just the two of you. *(Flatly)* Terrific. Yes, there's lots of room. We put up twenty CIA agents here last week. Never mind. Okay, come any time. The address is 18 Jacka Avenue. Jacka. The Aboriginal for bourgeois. You go along Palm Beach Road, through Bilgola, turn right into

Sunnyside Crescent, then left into Jacka. Yeah. All right.
Goodbye Paul.

(She hangs up and pauses, deep in thought.)

PETER: What is it?
CORALIE: Oh, nothing. Just some old friends. A bloke I
    used to live with and his wife. They're up from Melbourne,
    they're coming to stay here.
PETER: How long is it since you lived with him?
CORALIE: Five years.
PETER: Well, that's all right then, isn't it?
CORALIE: Yes.
PETER: Was it messy when you split up?
CORALIE: Very clean. I have the right to demand perfec-
    tion from a relationship. No less. I have that right.
PETER: Of course. Let me know when you've thought over
    my offer.
CORALIE: Look, what is this? What's so important about
    this party? Why are you asking me?
PETER: I thought it would be fun if we had a . . . date.
CORALIE: Fun for whom?
PETER: Mutual pleasure.

*(CORALIE looks at him. She laughs. PETER smiles.
JILL LANSDOWNE enters, through the side door, right.
She carries a basket.)*

CORALIE: Well, look what crawled out of the sea.
JILL: Oh. Sorry. I didn't know you were working tonight.
    I'll come back later.
CORALIE: All right, I deserved that, and more. There's a
    worm in my brain. Peter York from next door, my sister
    Jill.
JILL: Hi.
PETER: Can I get you a drink?
JILL: Thanks.

(PETER prepares her a drink at the bar.)

It was beautiful down by the beach. Not much wind, the
air was like a cloak, and the patterns in the water were out

of this world. It was great. I'm so glad I came down. I'm living fully again.

PETER: Why do you live in Canberra?

JILL: For my job.

CORALIE: For her ambitions.

JILL: I'm in the Public Service, administering the House of Representatives. Nothing special.

CORALIE: Stepping stones never are.

JILL: What she means is there's a possibility I may become secretary to a Minister—I mean, a real secretary, not a crypto-bunnygirl. I came down here for a few days to think over the offer. What's doing, ma'am? Are you going out? Have you eaten?

CORALIE: Sort of. I won't be going anywhere tonight. A couple of acquaintances of mine are coming to stay.

JILL: Oh. Will there be room?

CORALIE: Of course there'll be room. This is a mansion. What do you mean, will there be room?

JILL: Oh, just wondered. Who's coming?

CORALIE: Paul Coleman.

JILL: Who?

CORALIE: You met him. One of my mistakes.

JILL: Oh yes, I remember him. A vaguely cunnilingual turd with big thick lips. Yuk!

CORALIE: His lips are not thick. They're thin.

JILL: Sort of mean and evil.

CORALIE: Well defined. Attractive.

PETER: I'm getting a mental picture of him already.

JILL: Who else?

CORALIE: Look, what are you, the maitre d?

JILL: Just interested.

CORALIE: His wife Anne.

PETER: A short tall girl, clean shaven.

CORALIE: That's enough. Actually, I know Anne. Well, I met her once or twice, briefly. She's English, a gaminesque harridan from some provincial ghetto called Finsburystead-upon-Harrowfordgate or something. Two swans and a marmalade factory—it's very picturesque. Doesn't stop her from being slightly on the smarmy side, though. She's a film buff—always rushing off to see *Man's Favourite Sport* or discussing Guilt in Fritz Lang. Am I being unkind?

JILL: Very. But don't let that stop you. Anyway, you're jealous of Anne, that's why you don't like her.

CORALIE: If we could disregard that pubescent diagnosis for the while, we could possibly recognise that I dislike pretension, purely and simply.

JILL: You're against her because she married Paul.

CORALIE: Jesus! Jill darling, there are many things I'm against—capital punishment, racism, Morris West, pollution, but dear little Anne? No sir. I don't begrudge her Paul. When I met her I didn't see red, I saw vermilion, and I understand that's how it's turned out for them.

JILL: Ma'am, that is bullshit.

CORALIE: My sister. Yunnow, I've tried, I've really tried to do everything for this girl. What a story! Father dead, mother a fuckwit, grew up in Jannali with pimples and a concave chest, a tomboy at three, left at the post at twelve, latterly a failed political groupie . . . what am I hoeing into you for? Jill, I'm sorry. I mean, oh shit!

JILL: Coralie's being gracious.

CORALIE: I'm sorry, Jill, I'm so cruel sometimes.

JILL: I knew it couldn't last.

CORALIE: What?

JILL: You didn't talk about yourself for all of two minutes.

CORALIE: Jill, please, I'm sorry.

(Much grimacing and wincing from CORALIE.*)*

JILL: Okay, ma'am. *(To* PETER*)* Nothing like a bit of mild familial bloodletting.

PETER: Oh, don't mind me. I'll just sit around and suck ice cubes.

CORALIE: Don't be silly, Peter. Help yourself.

*(PETER *goes to the bar.)*

JILL: If you two want to . . . well, I might go for a drive.

PETER: Not at all.

CORALIE: Peter just dropped in to ask me to an Australia Party party. I haven't handed down my decision yet.

JILL: You're a politician?

PETER: A lawyer with an interest in sanity.

JILL: And the Australia Party fulfils your needs?

PETER: Oh, on all levels. If peace of mind can be defined

as the ability to relax in the company of mediocrities, then I've achieved a state of beatitude with the Australia Party. The poor buggers are so chronically progressive.

JILL: Good for them.

PETER: *(looking at her, then turning to* CORALIE*)* Well, I'm glad to see the Lansdowne family boasts at least one bona fide radical.

CORALIE: Don't you believe it. My little sister is heavily into the success ethic. She'll bury us all.

JILL: Just because I don't sit around all day on my big fat arse.

CORALIE: Anyway, you can't blame the poor girl. It's only a form of compensation.

JILL: Compensation for what?

CORALIE: *(going to the stairs)* I'm going up to wash my face.

JILL: Compensation for what?

CORALIE: Back in a minute. If Paul and that elfin charmer he married should happen upon us, then give me a yell.

*(*CORALIE *goes up the stairs.)*

JILL: Going up to change, are you ma'am? Going to make yourself look presentable?

CORALIE: *(leaning on the bannister)* No, actually, I thought I'd be tactful and leave you and Peter alone. So you can discuss politico-economic realities. Have fun, kids.

*(*CORALIE *exits upstairs right.* JILL *pours herself another drink.)*

JILL: Bloody bitch. You like Coralie, don't you?

PETER: Well, she's . . .

JILL: Coralie's a cream puff. Don't let all that aggression get you down.

PETER: I've seen worse. I wouldn't have picked you two as sisters.

JILL: We're a diverse lot. Mum, bless her soul, is a fuckwit. Dad was everything. The family. He held things together and brought us up. He was a very great man. Coralie and I worshipped him.

PETER: What did he do?

JILL: Oh, he was a kind of businessman. We had a roof

over our head, which is the best place for it. Can I get you something to eat?

PETER: No thanks. I had a snack. A bit of left-over pine-apple and risotto.

JILL: Have you got a family?

PETER: I'm divorced.

JILL: Oh.

PETER: I've got the house next door on my own. Tell me, do you and Coralie fight all the time?

JILL: Oh, I suppose we argue quite a bit. And seeing as Coralie's involved it's always on a completely irrational basis. She tends to lash out just for the hell of it. She's unfulfilled because nothing is ever good enough for her. Coralie used to hold us spellbound at the breakfast table with her plans for the day and then conduct lengthy post-mortems over dinner.

PETER: Was she ever engaged or almost married or any-thing like that?

JILL: Not really. There was Paul, but no, not really.

PETER: Would you say she was in any way sort of hostile to men?

JILL: That's the way it's turned out empirically. She won't compromise on any emotional issue. When she was younger, and let's face it, she's no teenager, she was the most incredible combination of romantic gooiness and perfectionism. If a bloke was ten minutes late he'd get the chopper. She imagines she has this gigantic sensibility which one day will be gratified and there'll be this great star-studded connection of two minds and two bodies meshing together and achieving life's high dharma amongst the peaks of ecstasy.

PETER: That's a tall order.

JILL: I'll say.

PETER: But she has changed, though, hasn't she?

JILL: Oh yes, I think so.

PETER: I do like her. You're right.

JILL: I've seen it before.

PETER: But it's no great hassle. I'll see how it goes.

JILL: If I were you, I'd—

(The door bell rings.)

PETER: That'll be the mythic Paul, I suppose. Shall I get it?
JILL: No. No, it's all right.

(She goes over and opens the front door. STUART
MORGAN *is there, carrying a small suitcase.)*

STUART: Hello, Jill.
JILL: Oh, hi. Come in.

*(STUART comes into the room. He puts down his suit-
case.)*

Put your suitcase over there, out of the way.
STUART: Oh. Righto.

(He moves it.)

JILL: Um, Peter, this is, uh, Stuart Morgan, a friend of mine
from Canberra.
PETER: And a very nice pair of lips you have, too.
STUART: *(startled)* Eh?
JILL: Private joke. This is Peter York, a neighbour.
PETER: And a human being, too, I hope. How do you do.
STUART: Hi.
JILL: Would you like a drink?
STUART: Are you sure it's all right? I mean, you know . . .
JILL: Everything's under control. Would you like a beer? I
got some in for you.
STUART: Thanks.
JILL: Sit down.
STUART: I'm all right.
JILL: Okay. I won't be a minute.

(She goes into the kitchen.)

STUART: I don't drink spirits. Only beer and wine.
PETER: Wise man.

(Pause.)

STUART: Is Coralie around?
PETER: I noticed her about the place a little while ago. She
can't have gone far.

*(CORALIE appears at the top of the stairs. She is nervous.
She hasn't changed her clothes, but has a bit of make-up
on her face. Her hair is brushed.)*

CORALIE: Paul? Is that you?
STUART: Hello, Coralie.

(CORALIE *comes down the stairs.*)

CORALIE: Who the hell are you?
STUART: Stuart. You know. Stuart Morgan, poet and public servant. From Canberra. You remember, when you were staying with Jill.
CORALIE: *(flatly)* Oh. Yes. You.
STUART: We had some good times. I've got fond memories of that Elgar recital at Bungendore. Anyway, how are you?
CORALIE: On top of the world. And you?
STUART: Not too bad. I just hitched down today.
CORALIE: Oh really. And how was it?
STUART: The last stretch was a bit frightening. I was nearly involved in a terrible accident.
CORALIE: What bad luck.
STUART: Yes. I hitched a ride with a semi-trailer driver and he was worried about falling asleep. "Talk to me," he said. "Tell me anything, tell me your life story, just keep me awake." So I started to tell him my life story and he fell asleep. Nearly went over a cliff.
CORALIE: What a pity.
STUART: Yeah. *(Looking around)* I like your humpy. The tree is of course fabulous. Do you have much trouble with leaves in the gutter?
CORALIE: I can't tell you. I just can't tell you.

(JILL *comes back with a glass of beer and a bottle for* STUART.)

JILL: Here we are. Oh, Coralie.
CORALIE: Yes.
JILL: You know Stuart.
CORALIE: Yes.
JILL: I must have forgotten to ask you. It's okay if Stuart stays for a little while, isn't it?
CORALIE: Yes, well, my reply to your anxious enquiry before still stands. There's plenty of room. He can have the den under the stairs.
JILL: It's not very big.
CORALIE: Neither is he. No offence.

STUART: I'm easy. Sorry you haven't had any advance warning.

JILL: That's my fault. I'm sorry.

CORALIE: No trouble at all. You and your paramour can have the run of the house.

JILL: My what?

CORALIE: Paramour. Lover. I got it out of Shakespeare.

JILL: Then you'd better put it back. Stuart is a friend.

STUART: I've come down for an interview with the State Public Service. About a new job.

CORALIE: Of course. You're a public servant. How about that, Peter? We have two public servants amongst us. Half the complement of our little gathering.

PETER: That makes this living room a microcosm, statistically speaking. Not that I have anything against people who work for the government.

CORALIE: The pragmatists. You two deserve each other. Actually, this reminds me of *Heritage*, a Charles Chauvel film about the founding of the Country Party—it's a tragedy. After society has been liberated from economic equality, the film fades out on the young lovers embracing on the steps of Parliament House, affirming the virtues of youth, love and wool subsidy. Sigh.

JILL: Stuart and I are certainly young, considerably younger than you, in fact, but lovers, no. That's the end of it. *(To STUART)* You'll have to forgive her. She's more than a little uptight about a visitor she's expecting.

CORALIE: You're up yourself, ma'am.

JILL: She's waiting with a pumping heart.

CORALIE: Like bloody hell. I got over that bloke years ago. He was impossible to live with. It just didn't work. Paul used to blunder home around dawn, reeking of perfume, alcohol, and his paramour's snatch. So I broke it off with him and never felt better. I went from screwing a phantom to laying a ghost and didn't regret a thing. In fact, I feel deep sympathy and understanding for Anne, knowing what she must have to put up with.

JILL: Easy, stomach, easy.

CORALIE: Bugger you, Jill, it's the truth.

JILL: I'm sorry, ma'am, but I don't believe a word of that carefully prepared communiqué.

CORALIE: Jill darling, shut up.

(Pause.)

PETER: Well, who'd like some more Southern Comfort?

(The door bell rings.)

JILL: I'll get it.

(JILL opens the door. PAUL and ANNE COLEMAN come in. PAUL carries two bags.)

PAUL: Hi . . . uh . . .
JILL: Jill.
PAUL: Coral's sister.
JILL: Yes.

(PAUL puts down the bags and advances into the room, followed by ANNE. ANNE is in the last stages of a nervous and physical breakdown, but maintains a defiantly "pleasant" manner.)

CORALIE: Hello, Paul.
PAUL: Good to see you, Coral.

(He pauses, then kisses her on the cheek gruffly.)

You know Anne.
CORALIE: Yes.

(CORALIE and ANNE smile briefly at each other.)

Paul and Anne Coleman, this is Peter York, a neighbour.
PETER: *(groaning)* Not again. How do you do.
CORALIE: And . . .
STUART: Stuart Morgan, poet and public servant.
PAUL: G'day.
CORALIE: Would you like a drink? We've got mainly bourbon.
PAUL: Thanks, Coral.
ANNE: Thank you.

(CORALIE goes to the bar. Silence.)

PAUL: Well, don't mind us, go on with the orgy.

(He laughs.)

CORALIE: *(smiling)* We were just arguing about something or other.

PAUL: What was the subject of the argument?

CORALIE: Oh . . . a film we saw on TV—*The Blue Angel.*

ANNE: Really? Andrew Sarris said it was definitive in retrospect. What did you think of it?

CORALIE: I thought it was *just stun*ning. The street. The light. And Dietrich.

ANNE: Yes, it's very evocative.

PAUL: You look a bit out of sync, Coral. Hope we didn't take you too much by surprise.

CORALIE: Oh, not at all. I didn't expect you so . . . on time.

PAUL: Mum always said: "If you say you're going to be there, be there. And be there on time." She'd tell me: "I don't want to hear your excuses. You said you'd be there, so you be there."

ANNE: But darling, you're the most hopelessly unpunctual man I've ever met.

PAUL: You got any more ice there, Coral? I wouldn't mind a bit more.

(CORALIE puts some more ice in a glass of bourbon she is preparing and hands it to him.)

CORALIE: So. What've you been doing?

ANNE: Paul's got this tremendous job with American Express—Operations Manager for the Sydney office.

PAUL: It's just temporary. Nothing much. They're in a bit of a mess, and they've hired me to help them out.

CORALIE: But haven't you got your own travel business in Melbourne?

PAUL: Oh yeah. My partner's looking after it while I'm up here.

ANNE: One has one's fingers crossed. Still, it's a fantastic opportunity for Paul.

CORALIE: Yes, I'm glad to see him doing well. He's come a long way from Marist Brothers, Mosman.

PAUL: But I still polish my own shoes.

(He laughs.)

CORALIE: When I knew him he used to polish his own

trouser seats. Anyway, you're welcome to stay for as long as you like. You can have the Fireman Suite up there on the mezzanine. You'll find everything laid on. Where are the kids?

ANNE: Paul's mother's looking after them, which is beaut. You've never seen them, have you?

CORALIE: No, I've never had the pleasure.

ANNE: I'll show you a photo.

CORALIE: Terrific.

(ANNE gets a photograph out of her handbag and shows it to CORALIE.)

ANNE: There's Joanna, on Paul's knee, and that's Tamsin.

CORALIE: Who?

ANNE: Tamsin. From Thomas Hardy. It's a Dorset variation on Tomasina.

CORALIE: Old Dorset, eh?

ANNE: Do you like the photo?

CORALIE: Oh. Yeah. Terrific.

(She hands it back.)

PAUL: Coral, we'll find a flat soon, don't worry.

CORALIE: Take your time. There's lots of room here.

ANNE: Yes, what a palace. And the tree is of course fabulous.

PAUL: We heard about your absentee American boyfriend and his bequest.

CORALIE: *(laughing)* All lies. But it was just what I needed. I've run to ground in my cliff-hanger hide-out.

ANNE: That staircase is just fantastic.

CORALIE: It gets me up and it gets me down.

ANNE: We just put in a new staircase at home. We've got this terrace house in Carlton and the old staircase was falling apart with dry rot and claret seepage, so we bought this spiral steel affair and put it up ourselves. It was quite a job—we rigged up a block and tackle on the front balcony, hauled this long steel pole into place in the stairwell, and then welded on the steps with an oxy torch a friend of Paul's lent us. It's a bluestone terrace, so the steel doesn't look too out of place. It gives us lots more room to move, which is beaut.

(Pause.)

I'm pregnant again.
CORALIE: Congratulations.

(Pause.)

PAUL: What about you, Coral? How are you getting on?
CORALIE: Well, apart from my caretaking responsibilities, nothing much. Just lying fallow, drifting.
PAUL: Just like when I first met you. You were at East Sydney Tech. Amongst the Art School Push.
CORALIE: I never belonged to the Push.
ANNE: Why not?
CORALIE: I didn't have enough Pull!

(She laughs loudly.)

(To STUART*)* Here, noisy, let me give you another drink.
STUART: Um, no thanks.
CORALIE: Get it into you!

(She fills his glass with bourbon.)

Yes, I saw the amount of wheeling and dealing, the heavy political shit that was needed on that in-group treadmill and I thought bugger it, if you have to trade in your tits you might as well be paid for it. I went to the beach instead. I was poor but honest and had a suntan.

(Pause.)

Things haven't changed much.
PAUL: Aren't you teaching any more?
CORALIE: No, I'm out of work. I've had it.

(ANNE considers this.)

ANNE: I find unemployment among teachers hard to understand. Surely if one is qualified one could find a suitably rewarding job.
CORALIE: What you say is very true. But sometimes some of us pedagogues feel the need to jack up.
PAUL: What do you do with your time?
CORALIE: Oh, this and that. I belong to a film group, actually. I've seen *The Five Samurai* seven times.

ANNE: You mean *The Seven Samurai.*
CORALIE: Yes. I've seen it five times.

(Pause.)

ANNE: That view looks just fantastic. I love those banana trees and that darling little bridge over the gap.

(She wanders out on to the terrace. STUART and PETER go to the bar, STUART to exchange his bourbon for beer, and PETER to stock up.)

JILL: It really is a beautiful view from the terrace.

(PAUL goes out to join ANNE. JILL and CORALIE talk quietly among themselves. PETER looks at STUART's discarded bourbon.)

PETER: Waste of good liquor.
STUART: I don't drink spirits. Coralie will have to learn that.
PETER: Oh? Why should she?
STUART: Because I'm going to marry her.
PETER: You?
STUART: Yes.
PETER: Does Coralie know about this?
STUART: Not yet.
PETER: I see, and you're going to sort of propose to her, are you?
STUART: That's right.

(PETER giggles. He is slightly drunk.)

PETER: Don't you think you might be biting off more than you can chew?
STUART: I'm not a lawyer. I don't bite people.
PETER: Forgive me, but I'm trying to picture it. I mean, Coralie's a . . . big girl.
STUART: Big tits.
PETER: Oh, absolutely, yes.
STUART: She doesn't faze me.
PETER: Well, if I hear an explosion that sounds like the end of the world I'll know you've put the hard word on La Lansdowne. Incidentally, good luck.
STUART: Thanks.

(PETER giggles. PAUL comes over to fill his glass.)

PETER: Is she giving you a bad time?

PAUL: Coral? Oh, she's all right. I've seen her in worse moods than this. I still don't know if what she needs most is a lot of loving or a well-aimed live telegraph pole in the region of her crutch.

PETER: But she's probably changed since you knew her.

PAUL: Not a bit. It's as if I left yesterday.

STUART: But she will change. I'm sure of that.

PAUL: Whatever you reckon. Bloody good stuff, this.

PETER: Yes, marvellous. I'm getting quite pissed.

PAUL: You're a lawyer, aren't you?

PETER: Lawyer, neighbour, these are mere labels. This man, I believe, is a poet and public servant.

STUART: Nothing more, nothing less.

PAUL: You look like death warmed up to me, mate. *(To PETER)* You sort of helping Coral through a bad patch, are you?

PETER: I take a paternal interest in the girl's welfare. After all, we're neighbours. Two solitary souls perched high above the Pacific.

PAUL: What about you?

STUART: I'm a house-guest.

PAUL: Nothing more?

STUART: And nothing less.

PAUL: Jesus! Surrounded by smart farts. Here, let's all get pissed.

PETER: An excellent idea.

STUART: You blokes have got a head start.

PAUL: What are you drinking beer for? Bloats you up like a stuck pig.

PETER: Never been weaned, that's his problem.

STUART: You'll see the light. Your brains'll turn to putty with that stuff.

PETER: I look forward to that.

PAUL: I've had a hell of a day, driving up to Pokolbin and back, stopping every five minutes so Madam can get out and have a piss or buy some dill cucumbers and chocolate ice cream.

PETER: You'll have to pander to your wife's cravings while she's pregnant.

PAUL: I pandered to my wife's cravings and that's how she got pregnant. Come on, where's your glass?

(ANNE *moves away from the door.*)

ANNE: Oh, I almost forgot, how silly of me! We brought you a present, Coralie. Paul darling, it's in my bag. Would you get it, please?

(PAUL *goes over to the bag.*)

We drove up to the Pokolbin vineyards today and bought some raw wine. One puts it down for a few years and that's how one builds up one's cellar. It's there in my bag, darling.
PAUL: Righto, righto.

(*He pulls out an iron with curling pins. They scatter.*)

ANNE: Paul, please be careful. Those curling pins cost money and it saves going to a hairdresser.

(PAUL *brings out a bottle of wine wrapped in paper. He goes to* CORALIE *and gives it to her.*)

PAUL: Here you are, Coral. This is for you.
CORALIE: Thanks, I'm overwhelmed. The first present I've ever had from you. I'll treasure it.
ANNE: It's from both of us. Now don't open it. You must put it down.
PAUL: Why? Tell me why.
ANNE: So it can mature.
PAUL: Why not buy drinkable wine now that we know is good. This stuff could be shithouse and we will have wasted all that storage space.

(ANNE *smiles graciously.*)

ANNE: You're difficult, aren't you? You're difficult to get on with. You ought to know, Coralie, you used to live with him. You ought to know that it's not easy.
CORALIE: It was like drinking Fanta through a live eel.
ANNE: Well, I think we should build up a cellar and this is a start.
PAUL: Okay.

C

ANNE: It's very pretty up there, round the vineyards. We drove around them all and it was heaven without the children. It wasn't too hot, which was beaut. The only sour note in the whole day was when I lost my toothbrush. We stopped at this revolting Ampol service station and I went to the toilet, which was ghastly. The floor was awash with petrol and urine and I dropped my toothbrush in it. Urgh!

(Pause. She sits down.)

Paul, will you ring your mother and see if the children are all right.

PAUL: Of course they're all right. Jesus, you wanted to get away from them and now you—

ANNE: Are you sure your mother knows how to look after them?

PAUL: My Mum not know how to . . . Jesus!

CORALIE: You put your foot in it there.

(ANNE indicates a tall cylindrical metal vase on the bar.)

ANNE: Coralie, I don't want to sound difficult, but there's something about that vase that throws me completely. I wonder if we could do without it for the time being.

(CORALIE, a bit puzzled, puts the vase under the bar.)

Thank you.

(Pause.)

PETER: I must be going. Thank you, Coralie. Good night, everyone.

(General goodbyes.)

CORALIE: See you soon, Peter.

(She goes to the door with him.)

PETER: What about my . . . offer?

CORALIE: I want to say yes and I want to say no.

PETER: I have a world view which encompasses indecision.

CORALIE: You would. All right, yes, it's a date.

PETER: Marvellous. I'll be in touch.

CORALIE: I know you will.

(PETER goes out.)

JILL: He's a funny bloke, Coralie. He seems to sort of just hang around, doesn't he?

CORALIE: Well, he's by himself. And he's good company, so why not? He sustains me. He's a very cool, together man. He oozes equilibrium and reason and sanity and all those qualities Jill lost and I never had. When I want a bit of solace I drop in on him. When he's had a hard day and wants a drink, a bit of suppressed titillation and a good listener he comes over here. End of biased account.

ANNE: Has he only one eye?

CORALIE: Yes, he lost the other in a skin-diving accident.

ANNE: What a pity.

CORALIE: Oh, Peter's well off. Everyone around here is rich and deformed. It's a freaky territory—lots of Mercedes and wheelchairs, expensively dressed cripples and crutches and elegant ladies with only one real tit. Millionaires with limps or one arm, that sort of thing. Peter's a refreshing contrast.

ANNE: I didn't notice any cripples. They all looked pretty healthy to me.

(CORALIE looks at her. She stands.)

Where's the bathroom?

CORALIE: One goes up the stairs and then one takes the second door on one's right.

(ANNE goes up the stairs.)

PAUL: Are you feeling all right, Anne?

ANNE: Yes, thank you.

(She goes up the stairs and exits off the landing.)

JILL: You were very mean to that lady, ma'am.

CORALIE: It's my party and I'll cry if I want to.

STUART: Perhaps you misunderstood her intentions in giving you the present.

CORALIE: Listen, comedy relief, when I want your opinion I'll ask the dog.

JILL: Stuart, I'd better show you your room.

STUART: Oh. Righto.

JILL: Bring your bag.

(STUART *picks up his bag and follows her under the stairs left. She gestures him ahead of her and looks at* CORALIE *coldly.*)

Vicious fuckin' bitch.

(*She follows* STUART *out.*)

PAUL: So. All by yourself.

CORALIE: Except for shit-for-brains from the corridors of power. She's been staying here.

PAUL: But you're really all by yourself.

CORALIE: Yes.

PAUL: Surprised to see me?

CORALIE: A little, yes.

PAUL: I thought I might give you a bit of a thrill. I should have seen you long before this.

CORALIE: Oh, why? Surely Anne and Joanna and Sing Sing are a big enough handful.

PAUL: Tamsin.

CORALIE: Tamsin. Is she a rhythm baby?

PAUL: Don't be a pain, Coral.

CORALIE: Of course, Joanna wasn't, considering the unseemly haste of the posting of your wedding banns.

PAUL: We were going to get married anyway.

CORALIE: Oh, I know. The decision had already been made by your tyke matriarch of a mother and that Irish thug, Brother Brengun.

PAUL: Brendan. Listen, it was my decision to marry Anne. Now you live with it, okay?

CORALIE: Oooo. All right, then.

PAUL: Anyway, forget all that. I wanted to see you.

CORALIE: Terrific. Just name the dates and times. I'll be there.

PAUL: Coral, you don't know how good it is to see you.

CORALIE: (*leading him on*) I missed you, Paul.

PAUL: I move into a different gear with you. A part of me has always wanted you.

CORALIE: A part of you, eh? A part. Now let me guess, it's the part of you which responds to sunsets, rum-soaked tobacco and windscreens in the rain. The yearningly roman-

tic side of a responsible-but-unfulfilled businessman, husband and father. That part of you whose sensitivity has
been bludgeoned by an unfeeling relationship and seeks a
modicum of solace elsewhere. Well, I'm not going to be
the bunny, not at twenty-nine, so go and do your scaveng-
ing away from here.

(PAUL laughs.)

PAUL: Give it to me, Coral, get stuck into it. Actually, I
meant the part of me that thinks you're a good sport and
just wants to have a relaxing drink. Tell me, what are you
going to do when Rockefeller comes back?
CORALIE: Don't know.
PAUL: Still prone to sulking, I see. Ooohh, look at that
bottom lip thrusting out.
CORALIE: *(smiling despite herself)* Oh, shut up.
PAUL: Look, what I wanted to say to you was if you want
to go overseas or just on a trip I can fix it up for you. Big
discounts, you know?
CORALIE: You're the travel expert, now, are you?
PAUL: Yep. I've been everywhere. Even had a book published.
CORALIE: What book?
PAUL: It's about travel, various places around the Balkans
and the East. It's not an official guide telling you how many
pairs of underpants to take, or what the Armenian for
gonorrhea is, but it tries to give the reader an insight into
the people of each area and how they live and what their
customs are and so on. Plus a few personal observations.
CORALIE: You'd be good at that. You've always been able
to talk to people. Have you got a copy with you?
PAUL: I'll give you one.

(He goes to his bag and gets out a book.)

There we are. Do you want me to autograph it?
CORALIE: No, I don't go in for that sort of thing. It's a
handsome book. Terrible photo of you, though. Were you
constipated?
PAUL: No, I was thinking of you.

(They laugh. ANNE appears on the landing.)

ANNE: Paul, I'm going to bed. Bring up my bag, will you?

(PAUL takes up her small bag and hands it to her.)

You won't be long, will you?

PAUL: No.

ANNE: Don't be long. Goodnight, Coralie.

(CORALIE waves. ANNE goes into the left door on the landing. PAUL comes back down the stairs. CORALIE puts the metal vase back on the bar.)

PAUL: I'm having another drink. Like one?

CORALIE: No thanks.

(PAUL prepares his drink.)

PAUL: We'll go if you want us to.

CORALIE: Don't be silly.

PAUL: Anne likes you. She admires your strength and self-sufficiency.

CORALIE: Terrific.

PAUL: So do I. You won't be messed around with, will you?

CORALIE: Not unless I want to be. I seem to want to be.

PAUL: The only thing that depresses me, Coral, is to see you alone. I think you need someone.

CORALIE: I've survived for twenty-nine years on my own. With the warmth of my own body.

PAUL: That's a cruel thing to say.

CORALIE: You were there some of the time. But you're right about the self-sufficiency. Now you are. I don't have to do desperate things like getting on a crowded bus just to feel contact with people any more. I can sit out on the front slope and look down at the beach at all the bodies, see all that flesh roasting in the sun, and not feel a thing. That is an achievement.

PAUL: Look, when we were together, I know I bungled . . . I know I could have . . .

CORALIE: Let's not go into that. Anyway, it was fun. We had a few laughs.

PAUL: It was good, overall.

CORALIE: Yes. I've managed to bash it into some kind of perspective, along with a couple of other basics. You can't walk on broken glass any more with nothing on your feet

but mayonnaise. That's my current outlook, anyway. What are you grinning about?

PAUL: I was just thinking how very you you still are.

CORALIE: You, you, what am I, a sheep? Of course I'm still me. This is still my skin, I'm still in here inside it.

PAUL: I can hear you.

(JILL *enters.*)

JILL: Stuart's fixed up.

CORALIE: Did you tuck him in?

JILL: No, ma'am, I didn't.

CORALIE: This bright young pair have arranged an assignation in my house. Can you believe it?

PAUL: Shocking.

JILL: Where's Anne? Is she all right?

CORALIE: She's gone to bed, which is beaut.

JILL: What are you two doing?

CORALIE: Nothing much.

JILL: I'll bet.

CORALIE: Don't be ridiculous. We were just reminiscing.

JILL: You mean about when you lived together?

PAUL: Yeah, the good old days.

JILL: Was it like being married?

CORALIE: Not quite.

PAUL: We had an arrangement.

CORALIE: Hey, do you remember the time when we decided bits on the side would be brought into the open?

PAUL: *(laughing)* Bloody chaos.

CORALIE: Paul had been working as a builder's labourer all summer and he'd come home all fit and sweaty with a deep tan. Yummy. I regretted our arrangement, I can tell you.

PAUL: It never worked, anyway.

CORALIE: That time you picked up that seventeen year old girl at that big dinner at the Mandarin. Remember that?

PAUL: Yeah. I gave you the word not to come back before twelve and took her home.

CORALIE: And I had to sit there for hours drinking Chinese tea with that randy cretin from the bush.

PAUL: But what about when you came home. I was working overtime.

CORALIE: I kept my side of the bargain.

PAUL: There I was. Chockers. The poor kid was so embarrassed.

(They laugh.)

CORALIE: Serves you right, you bastard. No sense of time, no decorum, no propriety.

PAUL: Must be my background.

CORALIE: No education, that's Paul's problem. All those Fascist Marist Mickheads dinned into their charges was the three Rs: Repression, Regression and Recession.

PAUL: What was the girl? Relaxation?

(They laugh. JILL stares at the floor. CORALIE jumps up.)

CORALIE: Well, I'm going to bed. Everyone else, depending on where their heads is at, can sort things out for themselves. Goodnight.

(She goes up the stairs.)

PAUL: Goodnight Coral.

JILL: Night, ma'am.

(Pause.)

Would you like something to eat?

PAUL: No, I'm all right, thanks.

JILL: Do you think you'll stay long?

PAUL: A few days. I'd best look for a flat as soon as possible.

JILL: Won't American Express get one for you?

PAUL: They've got a lease on a few padded cells, but I couldn't live there, and it's no place for kids.

JILL: Why'd you come here?

PAUL: Oh, we always stay with friends in rotation when we come to Sydney.

(JILL looks at him.)

I thought it'd be good to see Coral again.

JILL: She's very unhappy.

PAUL: Yes.

JILL: Well, I'm going to bed. See you.

PAUL: Right.

(JILL *goes up the stairs. She stops on the landing.*)

JILL: Turn the lights out, will you?
PAUL: Okay.

(JILL *exits left.* PAUL *goes to the window and looks out at the view. He drains his glass and puts it back on the bar. Then he picks up his bag, turns off the living room lights and goes up the stairs. He stops on the landing, outside* CORALIE's *door. He hesitates, then puts the bag down.*)

Coral? Can I come in?

(*He goes into* CORALIE's *room, pushing the door to. The ground floor lights go on and* STUART *crosses and goes into the kitchen. He wears pyjamas.* ANNE *comes out of the left bedroom door on the landing, wearing a nightdress. She sees* PAUL's *bag and goes to the door to* CORALIE's *bedroom. She pushes it slightly ajar and looks in. Then she pulls it to, goes downstairs to the bar and pours herself a drink.* STUART *comes out of the kitchen carrying a sandwich.*)

ANNE: Oh!
STUART: Just having a snack. Did I startle you?
ANNE: No, it's all right. I couldn't sleep. It's so hot.
STUART: Can you hear the surf from your room?
ANNE: No.

(*Pause.* ANNE *sits.*)

That service station. Where we stopped today. There was a tanker there and we couldn't get to the bowsers for ages. The man who was serving petrol didn't seem to care how long it took. He told Paul to put out his cigarette and I went to the toilet and lost my toothbrush. And when I came back the tanker was gone and the man serving petrol said: "You have to watch how you go in there." (*Laughing gaily*) I said: "That's good advice but it's a bit late." Imagine! I could have drowned or been asphyxiated and his advice was too late. What presence of mind!
STUART: They're a bit slow out in the country.

ANNE: Slow! "You have to watch how you go in there."

(She laughs. Pause.)

STUART: Well, I'm going to retire. See you in the morning.
ANNE: Goodnight.

(STUART goes out left. ANNE smiles, hesitates, then goes up to the bar. She takes off her watch, her rings and a small pendant and drops them in the vase. She opens the glass door right. A light breeze ruffles her nightdress. She breathes deeply, relaxing. Then she goes out the door.)

FADE OUT

INTERVAL

SCENE TWO

One thirty the following Friday afternoon. A hot, sunny day.
There is a stain on the tree trunk. CORALIE enters through
the glass door, right. She wears a bikini and carries a towel,
a basket and a spray of leaves. She goes into the kitchen, fills
a vase with water and re-enters. As she moves about she
sings to herself.

CORALIE: *(singing)* And now it's Judy's turn to cry
                 Judy's turn to cry
                 Judy's turn to cry-y-y
                 'Cause Johnny's come back
                 Come back
                 To me bar dumpah bahm . . .

(She is arranging the spray in the vase on the sideboard
when STUART enters, puffing. He wears swimming trunks
and a casual shirt.)

STUART: You beat me!
CORALIE: I took a short cut. Isn't this a beautiful spray?
  Flowers tend to leave me cold, especially when they're
  clustered in posies and bunches, but I love sprays of
  leaves, the way they lift a room.

(She is leaning over, concentrating on the leaves. STUART
admires her from behind.)

STUART: Yeah, they're great. I feel hot again.
CORALIE: Do you? I feel good. The water was lovely.
STUART: Yes, but the climb up the hill, that was murder.
CORALIE: You poor thing. I felt so sorry for you when
  that lady in the wheelchair ran over your sandcastle.
STUART: Well, what a bastard of an act.
CORALIE: *(laughing)* You should have seen the expression
  on your face!
STUART: I was upset, and rightly so. You build a structure
  from the foundations up, you plan, you extend, you decor-
  ate, and what happens? A rich bitch in a wheelchair runs
  all over it.

(CORALIE giggles and ruffles his hair.)

CORALIE: Oh, stop being so pretentious. Actually I was intrigued by those two angels of death in white coats who were helping her. I wonder if they're kept men? I've always wanted an occidental house-boy.

STUART: I'm a bit thirsty.

CORALIE: That bloody dog's pissed on my tree!

(She examines the stain on the tree trunk. She rushes to the sideboard drawer and gets out a hair dryer.)

Jesus F. Christ! Turn your back for five minutes and what happens? Rack and ruin, buggeration all round. Things fall apart, the centre cannot hold. Oh, my tree, my tree, my beautiful tree, light of my life, my tree, my tree!

(She plugs in the hair dryer, turns it on and rushes to the tree. She aims the dryer at the stain, but to no avail. She turns it off.)

Bloody thing. It's so ugly.

STUART: Don't worry. It'll fade away.

(She goes to the sideboard and gets a carving knife. She cuts off the bark with the stain and drops it in the waste paper basket.)

CORALIE: There we are. I couldn't bear it.

STUART: You're not going to leave it like that, are you?

CORALIE: What do you mean?

STUART: The tree will die unless you bathe the wound.

CORALIE: What with?

STUART: Olive oil and egg whites should do it. Have you got any?

CORALIE: I hope so. I'll look.

(She makes for the kitchen. STUART laughs.)

What's so . . . oh, you bugger!

(She throws a cushion at him.)

STUART: Sorry. I couldn't resist.

CORALIE: You don't deserve it, but would you like some lunch? A salad?

STUART: Yes, thanks.

CORALIE: You set the table while I get things organised.

(STUART sets the table. CORALIE goes into the kitchen, humming to herself. She comes out with two plates for the table, singing.)

> All alone am I
> Ever since your goodbye.

I was going to be a singer once, did I tell you?

STUART: No, you didn't. Sort of like Janis Joplin, eh?

CORALIE: I should say not. Frightening woman. The idea of being found dead in a hotel bathroom. Yuk! No, I was going to be just like my childhood heroine, Brenda Lee— well, a bit taller.

(CORALIE sings into an imaginary hand mike, with much flicking of the cord.)

> All alone am I
> Ever since your goodbye
> All alone
> With just the beat of my heart
> People all around
> But I don't hear a sound
> Just the lonely beating
> Of my heart.

(She bows her head.)

STUART: Great lyrics.

CORALIE: They express a great sentiment. And what about my idol, Lesley Gore.

(She sings.)

> Sunshine lollipops and rainbows
> Everything that's wonderful is—

Oh God, no. It's no use.

(CORALIE shudders.)

STUART: Are you all right?

CORALIE: I can feel night over my shoulder. We're here in the middle of the day and the sun is warm but I can feel night over my shoulder.

STUART: Come on, you'll be all right.

CORALIE: For four days now I've been seeing Anne's face in my mind's eye. And her body when they fished it out of the sea.

STUART: Yes, it was very sad, but let's try to—

CORALIE: That poor girl! That poor bloody girl! Paul was just sitting on my bed talking to me.

STUART: Now look, just try to keep calm.

CORALIE: Okay, okay. You're right. Calm.

STUART: Calm.

CORALIE: I remember when my father died I managed to shut out the pain for hours on end. Found all sorts of things to take my mind off the pain.

STUART: You're doing very well this time, too.

CORALIE: Oh, this is different. And besides, you've been rallying round.

STUART: I do what I can.

CORALIE: You've been marvellous. It's such a relief to be with a man who doesn't want to force me into anything. Peter and Paul are always laying heavy numbers on my head, and elsewhere. Always trying to make me play a role, and a supporting one at that. Brenda Lee would never have stood for it.

STUART: Well, you shouldn't let them bully you.

CORALIE: Oh, I have the odd horseshoe in my boxing glove. Anyway, it's not them I'm worried about, it's Anne. She's dead and I can't get her out of my mind. I can't.

STUART: Look, you heard what Paul said. She would have done it anyway. It wasn't anything to do with you. She had nowhere to go, she was dragged down.

CORALIE: I'm so cruel.

STUART: You're not cruel. Not at all.

(He puts his arm around her. Pause. She notices.)

CORALIE: What are you doing?

STUART: Putting my arm around you.

CORALIE: Well, don't.

STUART: Why not?

CORALIE: Because I don't want you to.

STUART: That's no answer.

(He kisses her and puts his hand on her breast. She pushes him away violently, and jumps up.)

CORALIE: *(angrily)* What the hell do you think you're doing?

STUART: Come on, Coralie. Come on.

CORALIE: I don't believe it. You've got the nerve to try and . . . and . . .

STUART: What's so unusual?

CORALIE: You . . . you . . . worm. You little bastard. How dare you! I let you stay here and bludge off me, I treat you like a friend, and what happens? How dare you!

STUART: Coralie, I love you.

CORALIE: What? ? ?

STUART: I want to marry you.

(CORALIE gapes at him. She tries to laugh.)

I'm not joking. The main reason I came here was to see you again. I really do love you. And I think you need me.

CORALIE: I can't believe I'm hearing this.

STUART: I think you're beautiful and devastating and so honest and you feel so strongly about everything, and you're vulnerable and passionate, and you've got dignity and some kind of solar energy inside you and you're a magnificent bitch with such ideals and . . . I'm not expressing this very well.

CORALIE: Oh, on the contrary, I get your drift.

STUART: I'm asking you to marry me.

CORALIE: How ridiculous! How dare you speak to me like that!

STUART: Coralie—

CORALIE: Christ, what a fate! What an inglorious end! Ambushed by an insect.

STUART: Look, who are you? What makes you so grand? What have you achieved?

CORALIE: You want a list of bourgeois accomplishments? Go somewhere else.

STUART: I see. You're just naturally grand, is that it?

CORALIE: Standing beside you I am.

STUART: The fact that I'm a bit shorter than you . . .

CORALIE: A good deal shorter.

STUART: . . . doesn't mean that I'm not worthy of you.

CORALIE: You're not worthy of anyone. Go and find a female worm and leave me be.

STUART: I'm asking you to marry me. What do you say?

CORALIE: No! No! I say no to the worm. I tell the worm to piss off out of it. No! Oh, I want to, I want to hit you!

STUART: Just as I thought.

CORALIE: No! Do you understand that, you treacherous little pipsqueak. You worm. I say no! *(Rushing to a window and yelling out)* I say no! No! I spurn the worm! I want out! I tell the worm to piss off!

(STUART looks out of the next window.)

STUART: Those people way down there on the beach. They're looking up at you.

CORALIE: *(shouting)* I'm Coralie Lansdowne and I say no!

STUART: They're waving. *(Waving)* G'day there! How are you?

CORALIE: *(turning on him)* You prick! Get your things and get out of here and don't ever come back. Ever!

STUART: Look, just take it easy.

CORALIE: Shut up! Shut up!

STUART: Look, Coralie . . .

(He advances on her.)

CORALIE: Don't come near me!

STUART: Let me make two points. One: you're aggressive and hostile towards men. Two: you've got an idealised relationship in mind which is impossible.

CORALIE: Let me make three points. One: you're a supine fuckwit. Two: I am aggressive towards you but not towards men. Three: get the hell out of here.

STUART: It won't do, Coralie. I've tracked you down. You haven't got a chance.

CORALIE: You can't track me down. I'm a big high-flying bird. I'm bigness. I'm greater than you.

STUART: Cut it out. You're just a twenty-nine year old unemployed teacher with big tits. You're also fatter round the hips and arse than you were a few months ago.

CORALIE: Get away from me. Get out of here.

STUART: You're a paper tiger, full of bullshit.

CORALIE: No!

STUART: I'll give you time to think it over, but I know what your answer will be.

CORALIE: I'm bursting. I'm bursting out of the top of my head.

(She slumps on the stairs.)

STUART: What are the alternatives? Where do you go from here, Coralie? Answer me.

CORALIE: Leave me alone.

STUART: Just look at yourself. What are your choices?

CORALIE: I'm a . . . I'm a . . . high-flying bird . . .

STUART: What a pathetic illusion. All you've done, all your life, is describe a small spiral inside a vacuum. A collection of tiny arcs. How much longer can you go on?

CORALIE: *(weakly)* No . . .

(The door bell rings. STUART goes to the door and opens it. PAUL comes in.)

STUART: Oh. Paul.

PAUL: G'day.

(CORALIE heaves herself up and goes up the stairs as PAUL comes into the room.)

Coral?

CORALIE: *(muffled)* Back in a minute.

(She goes into her bedroom.)

PAUL: Is she all right?

STUART: She's fine. What about you?

PAUL: I got the afternoon off. They've been very good. What are you doing here?

STUART: Oh, I'm still on leave, and Coralie said I could stay on for a little while. Is there anything I can do for you?

PAUL: No.

(Pause. He looks out the window.)

It's great up here. The drive was amazing. All those used car lots and sun-tanned birds and fish and chips and real estate offices. I never really noticed before. But now it was sticking into my eyeballs. And when you get up here it changes into trees and bananas and flowers and cripples. I love it up here.

D

(Pause.)

Mum's been so good. And my sister Gabriel. I couldn't tell the children. I had to leave the room. I went down to the back fence and cried for an hour. Jees I came close to . . . jees it was close.

STUART: Paul, if there's anything I can do. Is there anything you want done that you don't want to cope with at this stage?

PAUL: Thanks. I'll let you know.

(JILL comes in the front door with a shopping bag.)

JILL: *(to STUART)* Hi. Paul, how are you?
PAUL: I'm okay, thanks love.
JILL: If you want a baby-sitter I'd be glad to help out.
PAUL: It's okay, thanks. Mum's taken charge.
JILL: Righto, but give me a yell, you know?
PAUL: Yeah. Thanks.

(JILL takes a pot-plant out of her shopping bag.)

JILL: Look what I got down at the shops.
STUART: What is it, a thistle?
JILL: It's a bonsai plant, stupid. A fully grown live pine tree in miniature. They cut back the roots. Isn't it beautiful? I'm going to take it home with me.

(She puts it on the bar. Pause.)

Well, I think it's beautiful.

(She goes into the kitchen with her shopping bag. CORALIE comes out of her bedroom and briskly down the stairs.)

PAUL: Coral, I got the afternoon off. I thought we could—
CORALIE: Let's go.
PAUL: Well, what do you—
CORALIE: Come on.

(She goes out the front door. PAUL looks at STUART and shrugs.)

PAUL: See you.
STUART: Right.

(PAUL *goes out the front door.* JILL *comes out of the kitchen.*)

JILL: Where's Paul?

STUART: Gone out with Coralie.

JILL: Oh. I thought that'd be on again soon. Well, what are you doing today?

STUART: Nothing special.

JILL: Want to go to the beach?

STUART: No, thanks. I've just been.

JILL: We could go for a drive.

STUART: I think I'll stick around here.

(Pause.)

JILL: You know, I've never seen any of your poems. Why don't you let me have a look at some, or perhaps you could read a couple out loud.

STUART: I didn't bring them with me.

JILL: You don't know any off by heart?

STUART: No, I'm afraid not.

JILL: Oh.

(Pause.)

I started writing poetry when I was thirteen. I thought it'd be a bit superficial to rely solely on my looks so I thought I'd have this surprise element at work, where I'd be good at basketball, a genius at Maths, but really very aesthetic when you got down to bedrock. You know what I mean?

STUART: Oh, absolutely.

JILL: My first effort was called *Mozzarella Odyssey*, in which the poet—that's me—envisages herself as a pizza floating down a storm water channel the morning after cracker night when the acrid smell of cordite was upsetting the seagulls. I—the pizza—lose all my olives and anchovies and finally get emptied out into the sea.

STUART: What happened? Did you get eaten by an Italian shark?

JILL: No, the sea symbolised eternity and the poem ended in three dots.

STUART: It's an interesting device, three dots.

JILL: I suppose this must sound a bit naïve to you.

STUART: Not at all. Adolescence is entirely valid. Well, I think I'll go and catch up on my correspondence.

JILL: There's a good film on TV.

STUART: Oh?

JILL: Yes, on Movie Matinee on Channel Ten. *The Deep Blue Sea*. Let's watch it, shall we? Sit down.

(STUART sits down. JILL turns on the TV set.)

It's real fifties British stuff but quite good. It started at one thirty so it's been going for fifteen minutes, but I'll fill you in. Vivien Leigh's left her husband to live with this pilot who's a sort of the-skipper's-gone-for-a-burton type and he's burst the sound barrier or something and he likes golf and she's sort of unfulfilled. They're in this grotty flat and she's tried to gas herself. Her husband's a judge.

(She sits on the sofa beside him, then jumps up.)

Not enough contrast.

(She turns the knob and sits down again, a little closer to STUART. They watch. JILL turns and looks at STUART. He stares at the screen. JILL folds her arms and looks out the window.)

FADE OUT

SCENE THREE

Nine o'clock on Saturday night. The bonsai plant has gone. The living room is empty. PETER, *in dinner jacket, comes in through the glass door left.*

PETER: Anyone home?

(He goes to the bar to get himself a drink and moves the metal vase. It rattles. He glances inside it. He empties ANNE's *watch, rings and pendant on to the bar and studies them.* STUART *comes out of the kitchen carrying a sandwich and a beer.)*

STUART: Hi. She's changing.

PETER: Oh. Good.

(He gets himself a drink.)

Nasty business about that girl.
STUART: Yes.
PETER: I was quite shocked. Still, she looked all in.

(He puts some ice in his drink and sips it.)

So Coralie's still single, eh?
STUART: Yes.
PETER: How do you rate your chances? Do you think she'll come round?
STUART: I think she will. It's a question of coming to terms, it's not a question of what you want to achieve in life, it's a question of settling for what's available and reconciling fulfillment to an appropriate deal.
PETER: What does Coralie have to say about all this?
STUART: Coralie's gone a bit funny. She slops around the house thinking up song titles. Her latest effort is *If There Ain't No Light In Your Bathroom Then You Got To Shit In The Daytime.*
PETER: How catchy.
STUART: But she'll come round. She'll come to terms. It's a question of survival and I don't rule out happiness.
PETER: You're a bit frightening, you know. You're like an aparatchik of the emotions.
STUART: That's better than being a green-keeper.

53

(PETER stares at him. CORALIE appears at the top of the stairs. She wears a worker's cap, a dicky front and cut-away jeans.)

CORALIE: *(in a little girl voice)* Has my date arrived? Is my escort here? Gosh, I hope I make a good impression.

PETER: What the bloody hell . . . ?

CORALIE: I was thinking, how could I dress to please tonight's assemblage. I thought you'd need a piece of ultra-nubile radical muff to water the mouths of your progressive colleagues.

PETER: Oh, for Christ's sake Coralie, grow up, you stupid bitch.

CORALIE: I was only trying to please.

PETER: Of all the sophomoric, asinine displays I've ever seen from you, this is rock bottom. Okay, I'm going without you. It would have been nice to have a young, intelligent girl who could—oh, bugger you, I'm going.

CORALIE: Peter. Please. I'm sorry. I've hurt you. I'm sorry. It seemed funny at the time, but now I feel like a real idiot. Please forgive me.

(PETER hesitates.)

I'll go and change. Will you wait for me? *(Pause)* Peter, we have something, and I'm sorry I've jeopardised it.

PETER: Okay.

CORALIE: Am I forgiven?

PETER: Yes, you're forgiven.

CORALIE: Terrific. I won't be a minute. *(Starting to go)* Oh, I almost forgot. *(Tossing an envelope at STUART)* A present for you, Stuart. A plane ticket for the earliest morning flight to Canberra. Understand? Back in a sec.

(She exits.)

PETER: One of these days I'm going to introduce that bitch to a red-hot poker lined with shark's teeth. It'll be a messy but long overdue event.

STUART: I didn't think she'd . . . a plane ticket? How could she? I thought I was getting along . . . I mean, she was coming round . . .

PETER: Bad luck.

STUART: I was seeping into her consciousness. She needs peace, solace, a state of dharma. She needs kindness. She was opening herself up to me. It wasn't a big connection, but I was drawing her out, annealing her, she was coming to me.

PETER: I'm sorry to see your plans in chaos.

STUART: Yes, I moved too quickly. That was a big mistake. A few more days of infiltration would have done it, and then I could have built from there. She'll be the loser.

PETER: Stuart, you're giving me the shits.

STUART: I'm sorry. It's a slap in the face. I don't know what to do. Can you imagine Coralie at thirty-five? She'll end up like Anne. Apart from the calculations, I just wanted to give her love.

PETER: You're really stymied, aren't you?

STUART: A plane ticket Poor Coralie.

PETER: I'm looking forward to tonight. It's going to be good. I haven't felt this alive for ages.

(He pours another drink. CORALIE appears at the top of the stairs in a simple, flowing dress.)

STUART: *(stunned)* Jees, I don't believe it. A dress!

PETER: That's more like it. Sweet sixteen, my teenage queen.

CORALIE: Y'se can all get fucked.

PETER: What a virginal charmer. I'm odds-on for a good-night kiss here.

CORALIE: Don't get too confident. This dress is a concession on my part. We are now back on even keel.

PETER: Fair enough. We'd better be on time or the politicians'll pinch all the food.

CORALIE: I think I'll tank up with a Southern Comfort first.

PETER: I gather you're not looking forward to the party.

CORALIE: We're not going to romp across the moonlight beaches of Polynesia and have Gauguinesque orgasms under the trees, but I'll accommodate myself. I won't be inconvenient. You can steal mah chickens but you cain't make them lay.

PETER: Don't take that attitude. You'll enjoy yourself.

CORALIE: I'll enjoy myself. I'll enjoy myself.

PETER: All right, have it your way.

CORALIE: Oh Peter, don't be silly. I'm only joking. God, you're touchy tonight. Thank you for inviting me. It should be terrific. Better than hanging around here with old Moth Balls.

(A car horn toots outside.)

(Calling out) Taxi, Jill! Pity she's going. I got used to having her around again.

(JILL comes out on to the landing and down the stairs. She carries a suitcase, a handbag, and a shopping bag. She looks very businesslike.)

Want a quick one before you go?

JILL: No, thanks. I won't keep the taxi waiting.

PETER: I'm sad to hear you're leaving us.

JILL: Yes, it's been fun, but I start work on Monday.

CORALIE: She's going to be Secretary to a Minister. What do you think of that?

PETER: Congratulations.

JILL: Well, goodbye Coralie. Thanks for everything.

CORALIE: Oh, Jill!

(They embrace and kiss.)

JILL: You look after yourself, ma'am, won't you?

CORALIE: Yes, and you too. I'll come down and see you soon.

JILL: I'll come up again as soon as I've got the job under control. That's if you'll have me.

CORALIE: Oh Jill, of course I'll have you. Now you write to me next week and tell me all the ministerial secrets.

JILL: There won't be any. I believe in open government.

(They smile at each other.)

CORALIE: I'm sure you'll be a big success.

(The taxi toots again.)

JILL: I'll have to go. Try to be good.

(She kisses CORALIE.)

Goodbye, Peter.

(They shake hands.)

PETER: Good luck.

(He picks up her suitcase.)

STUART: Goodbye, Jill.

JILL: *(briefly)* Bye.

(CORALIE goes to the door with her. PETER follows with the suitcase. JILL takes it off him.)

I can carry it myself, thanks.

(CORALIE kisses JILL and she goes out the door. CORALIE looks a bit lost.)

PETER: She's going to do very well.
CORALIE: Yes. Well, I suppose we'd better push off. How do I look? Are any more adjustments necessary?
PETER: You smudged your make-up.

(He takes out a tissue and dabs her face with it.)

You don't know where you are, do you?
CORALIE: Not really, but . . .
PETER: I help?
CORALIE: Yes, you help.

(She smiles at him.)

PETER: Well, let's go.

(She puts the glasses back on the bar. The front door opens and PAUL comes in. He looks around at them. Pause.)

PAUL: Entertaining again.
CORALIE: Uh . . . yes.
PAUL: I was at a meeting down the road. My boss's beach-house. It was all full of shit so I walked out. I wanted to see you.
CORALIE: Paul, I wasn't expecting you.
PAUL: What do you mean, expect? I wanted to see you. I came here. Let's do something.
CORALIE: I'm sorry, but I'm going out with Peter tonight.

PAUL: Him? What's he got to offer?

PETER: Uh . . . look, I like to avoid unpleasantness wherever possible, but in this case I feel some sort of prior—

PAUL: You're not serious.

CORALIE: Yes, I am, actually.

(STUART holds up a deck of cards from the bar.)

STUART: Why don't you cut for it?

CORALIE: You. Out.

STUART: Now hang on, I was only—

CORALIE: Out!

(STUART exits to his room.)

PAUL: I need you, Coral. I blew out of the meeting and came here because I've got to see you.

CORALIE: And I'm always on tap.

PAUL: Look, there's no schedule for things like this.

CORALIE: There never was with you.

PAUL: You're not exactly a robot yourself. I seem to remember—

CORALIE: That was five years ago, you moron.

PAUL: And now I walk in and you've got two blokes on your string.

CORALIE: Two friends. Well, one and a half.

PAUL: You're like a rabbit, hopping in and out of the cot with all and sundry. Don't talk to me about your well-ordered existence.

CORALIE: In actual fact I've spent days without end getting smashed with Wormy and the Pirate Man, neither of whom could be classified as giants in the field of erotica.

PETER: Now look here, Coralie—

CORALIE: Sorry. Sorry. Unconsidered. Top of my head.

PAUL: My car's outside. Let's go.

CORALIE: No! I'm not going to drop everything for the sake of your whims. There used to be something appealing about your unpredictability but now there's nothing to compensate.

PAUL: You're a truly nasty bitch. There used to be a bit of zing along with the malice, but not any more.

CORALIE: The way you treated me, the, the way you treated me . . .

PETER: I don't really feel any useful purpose can be—

PAUL: Shut up! Coral, let's get out of here. I want to be with you. We can work things out.

PETER: She's changed, Paul. She wants different things. She doesn't want to be knocked around any more.

CORALIE: What would you know about it?

PETER: I can see you. I understand.

CORALIE: You have no inkling of what I am or what I aspire to.

PETER: Look, I'm not totally insensitive. I can understand your aspirations. For example, you wanted to be an artist, paint magnificent, brilliant pictures and so on.

CORALIE: Art nothing! I wanted to be brilliant in life, do you understand that, brilliant in life!

(CORALIE turns her back for a moment and then faces them.)

We shall now address ourselves to a couple of realities. I am going out with Peter tonight and we are leaving now. I know you've had a rough time, and I am sorry to disappoint you, but this was arranged a week ago. Good evening.

(PAUL is undecided. He leans on the bar, and then notices ANNE's things. He picks them up.)

PETER: They were in the vase.

(PAUL stuffs them in his pocket.)

PAUL: Coral . . .

CORALIE: Paul, will you go, will you go?

(PAUL hesitates and then goes out slamming the front door. Pause.)

PETER: How do you feel?

CORALIE: I hope Paul will be all right. He drives too fast when he's in a mood like this. I should have let him—

PETER: He'll be fine.

(STUART comes out of his room.)

STUART: I heard a terrible noise out the front—

PETER: Everything's under control.

STUART: What happened?

CORALIE: Nothing. A hard rain's gonna fall on that long train runnin'.

STUART: Song titles again. That's a bad sign.

PETER: We were just going.

CORALIE: Yes. Love shouldn't linger, love shouldn't wait. Who needs forever?

STUART: I remember Astrud Gilberto singing that.

CORALIE: Right. A voice from the past. I like my past. I wasn't mad about it at the time, but I like it now. *(To PETER)* Come on.

(CORALIE goes out.)

PETER: At last! I got her out of here. See you.

STUART: Bye. Have a good time.

(PETER goes out. STUART finds a book and lies down on the sofa to read.)

FADE OUT.

SCENE FOUR

Late that night. STUART *is asleep on the sofa, the book on his chest. Silence.* CORALIE *appears in the right doorway. She stands there very still. She carries her shoes in her hand. When she starts to speak,* STUART *wakes up and looks at her.*

CORALIE: Night makes it better, you know. The whole area seems reasonably beautiful, the whole palsied landscape seems tangible when you're down by the beach looking up and you walk through the shadows of the bananas and there aren't all that many lights. The freaks are asleep. All the moaning has stopped. It's silent, like a ship in the night. I've been down on the beach and among the bananas. I've been there for hours. I left the party, left all the creeps to drink and talk and line up screws for the night. I left my "escort", he was far too charming, and he frightened me a bit because he really is serious and he does seem to want me for something I can't face at all. So I left and walked and walked and sat on the beach and looked at the outline, the rocks and gums, the cracked shells and clustered droppings with very few lights and the freaks within and I surged up inside because I wasn't really part of this design, this conspiracy. And the surging peaked and then sank inside and I lay on the sand and I thought of the party and him and what he wanted me to do and the more I thought and the deeper I got into the night the more blurred the landscape became and the hill seemed like floodlights through a skeleton and the humming got louder so I went for a paddle in the sea. And I tried to think and my thoughts were physically painful and I walked through the rocks and the trees, through the bananas and heard the odd snatch of freaky life as I hauled up the steps to the top, where the most frightening thing of all was that this house seemed almost comforting.

(She is by now sitting on the sofa beside STUART. *They kiss.)*

You'll have to treat me well. I must be treated well.

FADE OUT.

61

SCENE FIVE

Four o'clock the following Saturday night. PETER *drinks at the bar. He looks at his watch.* PAUL *comes in the glass door, right. He too has been drinking.*

PAUL: What are you doing here?

PETER: Oh, I want to see Coralie, actually. She's not home. I'm waiting for her.

PAUL: Where is she?

PETER: I don't know. I haven't seen her for a week. Not since she walked out on me at the party.

PAUL: I want to see her.

PETER: So do I. I'm keeping a bourbon vigil.

PAUL: I want to see Coralie.

PETER: Then both of us will have to wait until she comes home.

PAUL: Both of us, eh?

PETER: Yes, I think that would be the best arrangement.

PAUL: What's your interest now? Still paternal?

PETER: I like the girl, even if she did call me a pirate.

PAUL: Yeah, well you just stick to being a good neighbour.

PETER: I'll do just as I please. Would you like a drink?

(PAUL nods. PETER prepares one for him.)

PAUL: Have you been here all night?

PETER: Most of it. I went to see a film with some friends of mine, a couple we've, I've known for years. It was a good film, I suppose, but I didn't like it. Too harrowing. I really don't want to see anything too strong or too depressing any more. They don't tell me anything new, which would be the only compensation. So my friends said come back for a drink but I knew it would be the usual ritual so I said no and came here. No sense in going home. There's nothing there.

PAUL: You haven't seen Coralie lately?

PETER: No. Tell you who I have seen hanging around a lot. Stuart.

PAUL: That obnoxious little twat.

PETER: Yes, I thought his ostpolitik had proved a failure, but he's still here.

PAUL: Who is this turdlet? He says he's a poet but have you seen his poems? Has anybody seen his poems?

PETER: I don't know who he is and I don't believe a word he says.

PAUL: I can't believe he exists. If he's a poet, where are his poems? The whole thing's got me beaten. Coralie, where are you?

(PETER hands him a letter.)

PETER: This was on the bar.

PAUL: *(reading to himself)* Dear Ms Lansdowne . . . what? She's going back to teaching?

PETER: It's not definite. Obviously she's just made a few vague inquiries.

PAUL: But even to think of it.

PETER: Yes, it's a reversal of form. I've often suggested to Coralie that she ought to reconcile herself to the modest aspirations of our society, but she's always interrupted me and complained of headache, dizziness and nausea.

PAUL: What was she like last time you saw her?

PETER: At the party? Oh, she was lively and charming to start with—a smash hit—but then she withdrew into a corner and played mah jong for hours with the host's nine year old son Tarquin. When I tried to dissuade her she'd just smile beatifically and say: "Tarquin and I are at peace with the universe."

(PAUL shakes his head. They drink.)

How's your business going?

PAUL: What business? From what I can work out, the nuns are at Katmandu, the heads are at Lourdes, and the Jaycees are demanding their money back at Nairobi airport.

PETER: What about your partner? Wasn't he—

PAUL: Hopeless. He's hopeless. No, that's not very fair. He's an old mate of mine. I've got a highly individual way of working and he couldn't follow it when I left. The debts are enormous.

PETER: That's most unfortunate.

PAUL: I finish up with American Express in a couple of weeks and then I've got nowhere to go. I've got nothing. Except Coralie.

PETER: But you had her before.
PAUL: I've got a different set of values now.

(The phone rings. PAUL *looks at his watch.)*

That'll be for me. I booked a call to Germany. I knew I'd be here.

(He picks up the phone.)

Hello? Yes, Coleman speaking. Right. Hello, Walter? Paul Coleman. Yes, how are you? Good. Sun shining over there? Oh, well, good for skiing, eh? Listen, Walter, fact is I wanted to ask about that account you were going to give us. Yes. Well, fact is Walter, we'd appreciate it if you could push it through pretty smartly, you know. You what? Oh. Yes. Look, Walter, that's a bit disappointing. Yes. Oh, come on, Walter, be fair. I don't think that's being very constructive. Now hold on, Walter, hold on . . . arc you there?

(Pause. He hangs up.)

Bastard of a kraut cunt.
PETER: What are you going to do?
PAUL: Oh, I don't know. Bankruptcy, I suppose. They'll take the house, but who cares? Coralie's all that matters now.
PETER: What about your children?

(They drink. The front door opens and STUART *comes in, looking happy and preoccupied, laden with a pile of presents in coloured paper. He dumps them on the floor with a grunt. He is wearing a suit, and shoes which make him five inches taller. He goes out again without noticing* PETER *and* PAUL. PETER *and* PAUL *look at each other.* STUART *comes in again with another pile of presents, dumps them and goes out again. He reappears, staggering in carrying* CORALIE, *who wears a beautiful dress. She is laughing.)*

STUART: I'll make it. You watch me. I'll make it.
CORALIE: Careful, I'm not insured.

(They collapse on the floor with much laughter, giggling

and embracing. Then they become aware of PETER *and* PAUL.)

CORALIE: Oh, hi. What are you two doing here?
PETER: Waiting for you.
CORALIE: What, all night?
PETER: Most of it, yes. What's . . . what . . .
CORALIE: *(giggling)* I had a pressing engagement.
STUART: A date with . . . Destiny!

(They collapse with laughter. PETER *and* PAUL *are stunned.)*

CORALIE: Followed by a Black Banquet.
STUART: A Saturnine Supper.

(Much laughter.)

PAUL: What's going on? Where have you been?
STUART: We just got married.
CORALIE: And then we had a big reception with all the Morgan and Lansdowne hordes and whoever else we could muster at short notice. All the relatives would have preferred a church wedding, even my hypocritical agnostic uncle.
STUART: We got pissed on champagne.
CORALIE: But we're all right now. We drove back in Stuart's new car at twenty miles an hour.
STUART: And this is our loot. Piles of it. And there's more in the car. I'll go and get it.
CORALIE: Do you want a wheelbarrow?
STUART: She'll be right.

(He gets to his feet.)

CORALIE: No one believed I wasn't pregnant, did they?
STUART: No one on my side of the family.

(They laugh.)

CORALIE: Stop big-noting yourself. *(Hugging his leg)* And guess what? My mother likes Stuart. She thinks he's lovely.
STUART: Short, but lovely.
CORALIE: They all said: "But Coralie, he's so much

E

shorter than you." As if that matters! Anyway, what am I, a giraffe? But after they got used to the idea, they decided that Stuart was wonderful.

STUART: They were pleased for you.

CORALIE: And relieved. Especially my mother. She's convinced I'm now only a skip and a jump from the middle class waxworks. Oh, and you know what we did between the wedding and the reception? We went out and bought Stuart a pair of shoes. Show them, Stuart.

(STUART pulls up his trouser legs to show PETER and PAUL his five-inch heels.)

STUART: They're bloody killers, I can tell you.

CORALIE: If I'd been in bare feet we would have been a perfect pair. But alas, with my heels I was still taller than him. Never mind.

STUART: I'll get the rest of the presents.

(He goes out. Pause. CORALIE's smile fades and she looks away from PAUL.)

CORALIE: How are things with you, Paul?

PAUL: Coral . . .

CORALIE: Let's have a drink to celebrate my marriage.

(PAUL goes to the glass door, right. He shakes his head.)

Look, what's the matter with you? Are you going to get all . . .?

PAUL: Coral, you did it. You did it.

CORALIE: Yes.

(PAUL looks at her and then goes out. CORALIE steels herself.)

I married the man of my choice. Do you have any objections?

(PETER stares at her.)

PETER: You? And Stuart?

CORALIE: Yes, me and Stuart. What of it?

PETER: It's absurd . . . ridiculous . . . I have a world view which . . . *(Stumbling towards the glass door, left)* It's absurd . . . totally ridiculous.

(He goes out. CORALIE is still for a moment, then she goes over to the presents and looks at them. She picks one up and opens it. It is a Sunbeam electric frying pan. She looks at it. STUART staggers in with another pile of presents and dumps them on the floor.)

STUART: That's the lot.

CORALIE: Come and sit down and we'll open them.

STUART: Righto. I'll just take these shoes off first. I want to see if the floor's still there.

(He sits on the sofa and takes off his shoes.)

Ahhhhh.

CORALIE: Stuart.

STUART: Yes?

CORALIE: Come and give me a kiss.

(He goes over and kisses her. She has to bend down to reach him. She smiles at him.)

I don't care how tall you are.

STUART: That's good, because I'm not going to grow any more.

CORALIE: Come on, let's open the presents. This was the first, a Sunbeam frying pan.

STUART: You start at that end.

(They sit on the floor and start opening presents.)

CORALIE: I had a ball at the reception, actually. It was good fun.

STUART: Pink sheets with a curly design.

CORALIE: Yuk!

STUART: Yes, it was good, except for the food.

CORALIE: Oh God, yes. That lethal roast lamb. And the dessert! I can't think of anything more right-wing than Bombe Alaska.

STUART: A Sunbeam frying pan.

CORALIE: A set of barbecue cutlery.

STUART: I liked your mother.

CORALIE: Stop being diplomatic. We're home now.

STUART: No, I did. I really did.

CORALIE: Claggy harridan. What's that?

STUART: A car-washing gift pack with bio-degradable shampoo.

CORALIE: Look at this awful vase. Bet it's from Sandra. *(Checking the card)* Yes, I bet she got it for her wedding, the bitch.

STUART: You won't believe this.

CORALIE: What is it?

STUART: A Sunbeam frying pan.

CORALIE: Christ, what imagination. They all think you'll be cooking breakfast for me. I could see what they were thinking.

STUART: Everything turned out all right. We all got pissed towards the end.

CORALIE: Yes, when things got a bit lively I said to Betty —that middle-aged cousin of mine, I introduced you—the ovoid lady in the black hat. I said to her: "Betty, this is a vulture's banquet." And she said: "Why is that, Coralie?" And I said: "Because there's a lot of carrion on!"

(CORALIE laughs. Her laughter is softer and more musical than previously.)

Well, it didn't happen exactly like that, but you've got to laugh. What's that?

STUART: A toaster. You can get three slices in.

CORALIE: This feels like a record.

STUART: What is it?

CORALIE: Janis Joplin. That'll have to go.

(She tosses it away.)

STUART: Give me a hand with this one, will you?

(They open a box.)

CORALIE: A Sunbeam mix-master.

STUART: That'll be useful.

CORALIE: Speak for yourself.

STUART: Here's something simple. A cook book.

CORALIE: I just know what this is going to be.

(She unwraps a Sunbeam frying pan.)

STUART: Let's have a fried egg party. We can feed the masses.

CORALIE: I want another kiss and a cuddle.

(STUART kisses her. They roll among the presents, giggling.)

Ohh! My lungs have been crushed. *(Hugging him)* You're solid, aren't you? You're really solid. I bet you were good at football. Did you play football?

STUART: I used to play on the wing for University Rovers, actually.

CORALIE: I bet you were fast and good at tackling.

STUART: Well, I was fast.

(CORALIE giggles.)

CORALIE: Let's go to bed.

STUART: All right. But I'm not going to carry you up the stairs.

CORALIE: Then I'll carry you up. Come on.

STUART: No, absolutely not.

(CORALIE coughs.)

CORALIE: Oh come on, Stuart, don't be a bad sport. I can carry you.

(She coughs again.)

STUART: You'll have to catch me first.

(He runs around the sofa and she chases him with shouts of glee.)

CORALIE: Come back here, you little bastard.

STUART: I'm still fast. I was a flying winger.

(He runs halfway up the stairs.)

CORALIE: Now that's not fair.

(She coughs.)

STUART: Are you all right, Coralie?

CORALIE: *(coughing)* Just something . . .

(She subsides on to the sofa, wheezing. STUART runs back down and gets her a glass of water.)

STUART: Here, drink this.

(She tries to drink it but splutters all over the place.)

Coralie, what's the matter? Can't you speak?

(She gags, shaking her head.)

Did a bit of food go down the wrong way?

(CORALIE wheezes and moans painfully. STUART slaps her on the back, but it doesn't do any good.)

Jees, I'd better call a doctor.

(He gets the phone book.)

Have you got a regular doctor?

(She manages to shake her head.)

Hang on, there's one down in Sunnyside Crescent, at the bottom of the steps. What's his name?

(He flips through the Pink Pages phone book.)

What's his name? I've been past there a thousand times. I could run down . . . No, I'd better not leave you. Salmon! That's it. Here it is.

(He dials a number on the phone. CORALIE tosses on the sofa.)

Doctor Salmon? My name's Morgan and . . . my wife's in terrible pain. It's an emergency. She's coughing and gagging and she can't breathe properly. Eighteen Jacka Avenue. Look, we're just at the top of the steps if you go out the back. I can see your house from here. Ours is the one with the tree growing out the top. Good. Thanks a lot. Really appreciate it.

(He hangs up.)

He's coming right up. Can you hold on?

(CORALIE is breathing only with great difficulty. STUART makes her comfortable.)

Are you warm enough? Are you too hot?

(He takes off her shoes.)

Are your clothes too tight? Can I loosen anything?

(She manages to shake her head.)

I'll get you a cold washer.

(He rushes out to the kitchen and returns with a wet washer. He sponges down her face and neck.)

What a thing to happen on our wedding night! You'll be all right, Coralie, you'll be all right. Is there anything I can get you? Have you had this before? Have you got any special pills?

(She manages to shake her head.)

Coralie, I can't lose you now. Not after all . . . Coralie, you've got to be all right. Oh, hurry up, Doctor Salmon, hurry!

(He goes to the right door and looks out.)

Oh no! Oh jees!

(He comes back into the room.)

He's coming, but oh God! Still, how was I to know? I couldn't have known. He's a doctor, he must have done this before. Oh jees, what have I done?

(He comforts CORALIE.)

He's coming, Coralie, he's coming. Just hold on, darling. You'll be all right. You've got to be all right.

(Noises are heard on the terrace outside. STUART rushes over and opens the door.)

Doctor Salmon, do come in. I'm terribly sorry.

(DR SALMON limps into the room. He wears sunglasses, casual clothes, carries a black bag, has an artificial leg, and walks with the aid of a walking stick.)

DR SALMON: Mr Morgan?
STUART: Yes, and I'm sorry about, well, you know, the steps, and your, you know, coming up, with the, uh . . .

DR SALMON: She can't breathe, you say?

STUART: No, she's been coughing and wheezing. Can't talk. It's terrible.

(DR SALMON eases himself into a chair beside CORALIE.)

I'll get a cushion for your leg.

DR SALMON: I haven't got a leg. It was amputated above the knee.

STUART: Oh.

DR SALMON: Breathe in, dear.

(CORALIE struggles to breathe.)

Uh-uh. Now breathe out.

(She wheezes.)

STUART: See what I mean, she can't breathe properly. Could be food inhalation. Maybe it's a blockage in the larynx or the oesophagus.

DR SALMON: Thank you for your help, Mr Morgan.

(STUART retires to the bar.)

Now, Mrs Morgan, I want you to sit up. Here we go. Come on, dear.

(He hauls CORALIE into a sitting position.)

That's it. Steady.

(He brings a torch out of his bag and examines her ears.)

All right now. I want you to say "ah" loudly, breathing out.

(CORALIE gags.)

Come on, you can do it. Lean forward.

CORALIE: Ah.

DR SALMON: Again, and longer.

CORALIE: Aah.

(He slaps her hard on the back.)

DR SALMON: Again.

CORALIE: Aahh.

(He slaps her hard on the back.)

Aahhhh!

DR SALMON: Big one, big one.

(He slaps her.)

CORALIE: AAAHHHHH! ! !

DR SALMON: That's it. Now see if you can breathe.

(CORALIE breathes more or less normally.)

That's good. You're all right now.

(He writes out a prescription.)

STUART: What was it? Her epiglottis? Did any blood come up?

(DR SALMON writes.)

That was a bit scary there for a while. I didn't know what to do. She couldn't breathe properly.

DR SALMON: Here's a prescription for some antibiotics. There's a bit of inflammation in her upper respiratory tract. She should rest for a couple of days.

STUART: All right. Thanks, doctor.

(DR SALMON looks at the presents.)

DR SALMON: Just married, eh?

STUART: Yeah. What a way to spend your wedding night. Not a very good start, eh?

DR SALMON: That's the least of your worries. Goodnight, or morning, rather.

(He goes out.)

STUART: Bloody doctors. They never tell you anything. Poor darling. *(Kissing CORALIE on the forehead)* You had me worried. But you're all right now. What a night!

(He goes to the windows and doors and pulls back the curtains. Dawn light fills the room.)

Looks like a beautiful day. A few board riders out al-

ready. We could have some breakfast outside, if you feel up to it. Or maybe you'd prefer to go to bed.

(Pause.)

I suppose I'd better go and look for a chemist and get this prescription filled.

(Pause.)

Poor darling.

(Pause.)

You won't be able to go surfing for a few days.

(Pause. CORALIE stands up, a bit gingerly at first. She walks a few paces and stops. She looks around the room slowly and calmly and then her eyes come to rest on STUART. They stand there, looking at each other. Silence.)

CORALIE: You'll do.

(STUART looks at her apprehensively. Silence.)

FADE OUT

END OF PLAY

Other Currency Methuen Plays

Ron Blair
President Wilson In Paris

Alexander Buzo
Macquarie
Three Plays—Norm & Ahmed
Rooted
The Roy Murphy Show

George Darrell
The Sunny South

Louis Esson
The Time Is Not Yet Ripe

Edward Geoghegan
The Currency Lass

Dorothy Hewett
The Chapel Perilous

Jack Hibberd
A Stretch of the Imagination

Peter Kenna
The Slaughter of St. Teresa's Day
A Hard God

Jim McNeil
Two Plays—The Chocolate Frog
The Old Familiar Juice
How Does Your Garden Grow

Ralph Peterson
The Third Secretary

Katharine Susannah Prichard
Two Plays—Brumby Innes
Bid Me To Love

Betty Roland
The Touch of Silk

John Romeril
I Don't Know Who To Feel Sorry For

James Searle
The Lucky Streak

David Williamson
The Removalists
Don's Party
Three Plays—The Coming Of Stork
Jugglers Three
What If You Died Tomorrow

Brochures are available from

Currency Methuen Drama Pty Ltd
301 Kent Street,
Sydney, N.S.W. 2000

Wholly set up and printed in Australia for Currency Methuen Drama Pty. Ltd., 301 Kent Street, Sydney by John Sands Pty. Ltd., Halstead Press Division, 1974.